THE CARNIVAL
OF MARVELS AND MONSTERS

A MUSICAL TALE WITH CD
BY MIHALIS MAKROPOULOS

MUSIC AND LYRICS
Giannis Georgantelis

ILLUSTRATIONS
Katerina Veroutsos

Des mots plein la bouche

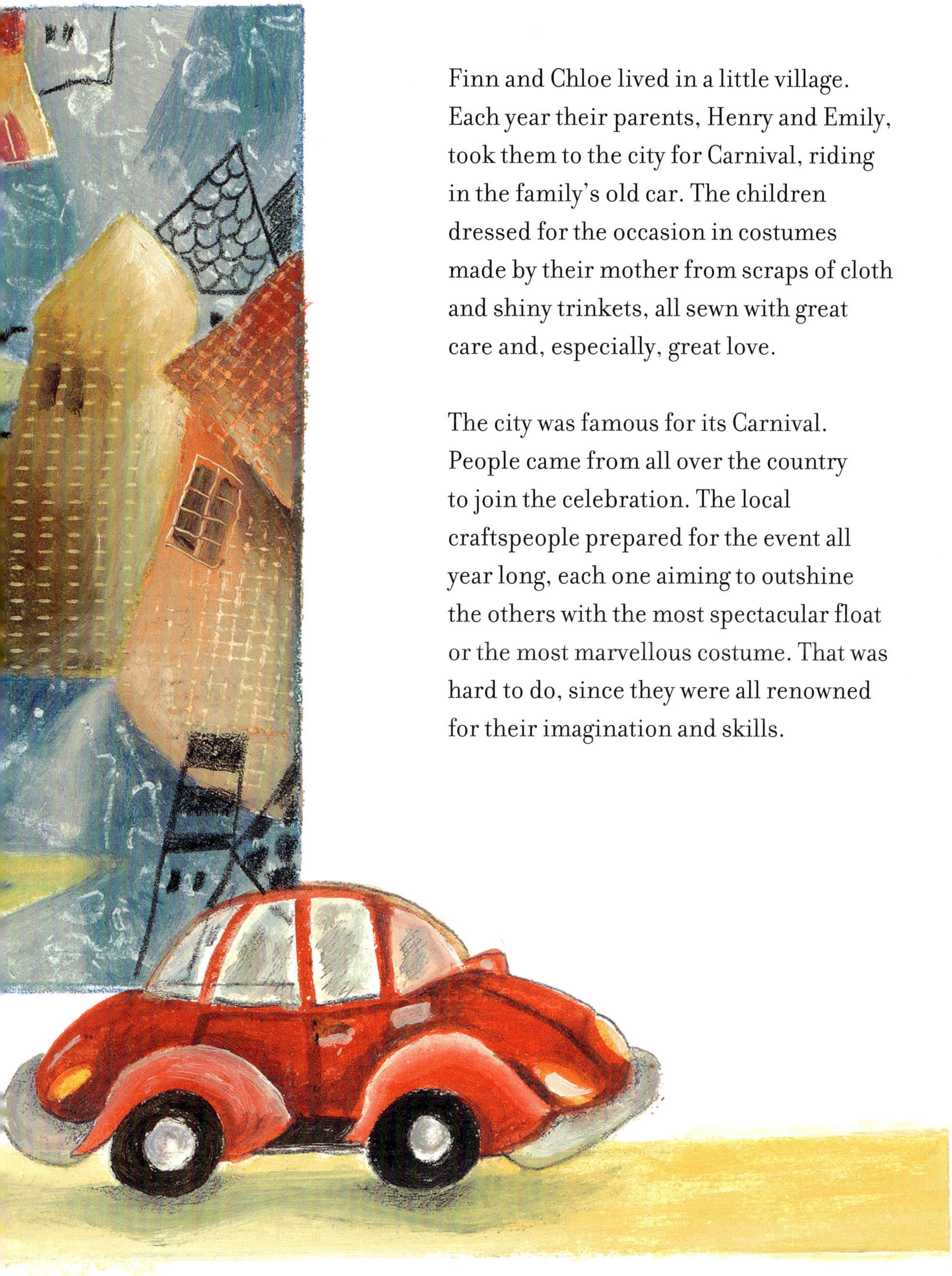

Finn and Chloe lived in a little village. Each year their parents, Henry and Emily, took them to the city for Carnival, riding in the family's old car. The children dressed for the occasion in costumes made by their mother from scraps of cloth and shiny trinkets, all sewn with great care and, especially, great love.

The city was famous for its Carnival. People came from all over the country to join the celebration. The local craftspeople prepared for the event all year long, each one aiming to outshine the others with the most spectacular float or the most marvellous costume. That was hard to do, since they were all renowned for their imagination and skills.

Carnival oh Carnival
Our every day is remarkable
So all year long we're feasting
Dragons, demons, goblins, creatures,
Lions, foxes, hares and seagulls
In our magic town are leaping

Who will be the fool and who will win the duel?
In this crazy hoopla freaky characters are prying
Who will be the mule and who will get to rule
In the darkness of our town behind their masks are hiding

People wearing masks and costumes
Gowns are twirling in the ballrooms
Celebrations are beginning
Crazy hats with crazy big plumes
Crazy parties in the classrooms
Look at those cats, they're grinning

Who will be the fool…

Carnival, that time again
Our charming city gone insane
The big parade is starting
Fairies, pirates, imps and robins
Parents, children even grannies
Singing, having fun and dancing

Who will be the fool…

The Carnival was hosted by a queen and a king: the Queen of Day and the King of Night. No one had ever seen their real faces, but it was they who organized the festivities and hired the tailors and seamstresses to make the costumes for their armies. The Army of Day was dressed as gentle animals and birds, the Army of Night as frightful monsters. The King of Night wore a dreadful demon mask, and his robe was so black that it swallowed every bit of light. Wherever the King went, darkness spread around him. The Queen of Day was masked as a kindly old lady, and her gown was so radiant that it wreathed her in sunshine.

Black or white, darkness or light
Something is waiting to scare you in the shadows of the night
Our city has miracles, monsters unbearable
Creatures who walk around
But when I'm beside you the night has no power
Just close your eyes
Everything's right

Black or white, darkness or light
Gremlins are shifting under your bed but can't bite
Because in your dreams I will visit you secretly
Riding a moonbeam tonight
Together we'll fly over rooftops, while goblins stay behind
Fly by my side

Even without the splendid fabrics used by the costume-makers in the city, Emily, the children's mother, always created wonderful outfits. This year they were finer than ever before. Eleven-year-old Finn was the Sky, with clouds and stars. On his chest was a glowing sun made of bits of glass and on his back, a moon crafted from shiny chocolate candy wrappers. Chloe, age eight, was the Earth. Her costume was adorned with flowers fashioned from odds and ends of colourful cloth and, here and there, tiny stuffed animals with beads for eyes.

Oh! your face it glows so brightly
From the golden rays of that big sun that you wore
Shooting stars are streaking through the night sky
Past Orion's belt you're walking on a distant shore

Your costume is magical and bright
It flies us far away beyond the stars
To a fantastic world of light, or else,
To a comet passing Mars

Oh! they look like they are growing
The many coloured flowers on the costume that you wear
Wild animals among them look like prowling
And you sing along as you fly up in the air

Your costume embraces all the earth
We travel in it as it spins around
To forgotten prairies back and forth
Or in a den beneath the ground

La la la....

That day, on the way to the city, the children quivered with joy and impatience in the back seat. The old car stalled and restarted. Over and over it threatened to break down in the middle of the road. Henry murmured soothingly as he made repairs, and by some miracle the worn-out jalopy continued to run. Finally they arrived, just in time. The streets were alive with music, packed with costumed revelers amid fluttering streamers and clouds of confetti.

"Be careful now, children," said Henry.
"Hold tight to our hands or you could get lost."

Just then, the terrible King of Night peered out from a dark alley and saw the children's costumes. Instantly, he flew into a rage. Even his best tailors, working with the world's most costly fabrics, had never managed to create costumes of such splendour.

The King summoned three of his demon soldiers, one with sharp fangs, one with menacing horns and one with blazing red eyes.

"Bring me those children dressed as Sky and Earth," he barked.

"But how?" cried a lurking creature with bulging eyes and no nose. "They're with their parents."

"Take them by surprise with smoke and flames," ordered the King. "Force the parents to let go of the children and then grab them!"

The ghastly demons obeyed at once. Hopping and prancing, they approached the family. The one with little bat wings on his back held a flaming torch. The second one carried matches and old rags, and the third gripped a fireplace bellows. The winged demon gave the signal by putting the torch in his mouth, swallowing the flames and then spitting them out like a dragon.

"Look, Papa," cried Finn, delighted. "He's eating the flames!"

With that, the second demon threw the rags to the ground and set them on fire, and the one with the bellows fanned the flames. Thick black smoke enveloped the little family. Henry felt Finn's hand slipping away, and Emily lost hold of Chloe.

"Henry!" she screamed, "the children!"

"Finn! Chloe!" called their father. "Where are you?"

He couldn't see a thing. Little by little the smoke drifted away and the parents reappeared, but the children were nowhere to be seen.

"Henry! We've lost the children!" cried Emily.

And she fell sobbing into her husband's arms.

Meanwhile, the demons had hustled Finn and Chloe to the King of Night waiting in a dark alley full of cats, which were all black, of course.

Black claws scratching, sharp teeth biting,
Sneaking there behind black fences
Bright eyes gleaming, shadows creeping
In between the tall black branches

Black and scary, black and screechy,
Black and creepy, black and clumpy, cats attack!
Evil, twisted, hissing, crouching,
Red eyes peering, demon feline, cats strike back!

Let's sing to life in pitch black

To the silver moon they're singing,
Screeching, horrid, tone-deaf meowing
When they try to fall asleep then,
Only dark black sheep they're counting

Black and scary...

The cats' yowling was horrible and the King's laugh was the most frightening sound the children had ever heard. But the demons were moaning in pain. Their captives were not shy! Finn had kicked two of them on the shins, and Chloe had bitten the third's pointy nose. She might be a little girl but her jaw was strong as steel.

What have we got here? So small and full of fear!
It looks like a young boy! Who's dressed so very weird!

A sun so bright I lose my sight, a moon that shines like silver
A sky so vast that drapes his dress, it gives me such a shiver!
I want to know the secret that's behind this magic costume
It shines and glows so beautifully, in the darkest night.

So what do we have here? So small and full of fear!
It looks like a young girl! Who's dressed so very weird!

A painted earth sewn on her dress with meadows full of flowers
And animals that come to life with eyes made out of jewels
I want to know the secret that's behind this magic costume
It shines and glows so beautifully, in the darkest night.

Bravely hiding their fright, the children stood in front of the King of Night.

"Who made those costumes?" he demanded.

"Our mother," answered Finn.

"What are they made of? Let me see! These flowers are just old scraps," sneered the King, trying to hide his jealousy.

"Yes, they are made from scraps, but with something else, too," said Chloe.

Ignoring her, the King of Night went on.

"And this sun, what's it made of? And this moon? Broken glass and chocolate wrappers?" He laughed again, this time with a grating sound that made the black cats lie flat and stiffen their whiskers like guitar strings.

The King's laugh sounded like rasping saws and buzzing wasps in the boy's ears, but he answered.

"Yes, they are made of glass and shiny wrappers, but with something else, too."

"And just what is this something else, my dear little ones?" asked the King in a soft, oily voice, hoping to get them to give up the secret his tailors could use to make costumes a thousand times more magnificent than theirs.

"The something else is our mother's love," said Finn and Chloe.

The King of Night was enraged.

"You're mocking me!" he shouted. "Lock them up in the costume room," he ordered the demons. "And put the cats in with them!"

Now, normally, a black cat is no more frightening than a white or a spotted cat, but these cats were darker than darkness itself, with coal-black eyes and hooked black claws.

The demons seized the children, who resisted courageously. But they were outnumbered.

"Sit down, dearies," snickered the bat-winged demon as he closed and locked the door. "The kitty cats will be here soon."

The costume room was very dark, but not completely. Hundreds of lavish costumes were hanging there, decorated with gems and pearls that shone in the dark like stars on a moonless night.

There is a room devoid of cheer
Silently costumes start to appear
Who's the one disturbing our sleep?
Who is daring in our space to creep?

They seem alive don't run away
Just turn your back, they'll start to sway
Who's the one disturbing our sleep?
Who is daring in our space to creep?

Chloe took her brother's hand.

"What are we going to do, Finn?"

"Let me think," he said. "Wait! I have an idea. We're going to tear all the jewels off these costumes and pile them up there, in front of the door."

"Why?" asked the little girl.

"You'll see."

Snatching the decorations as if they were picking cherries, the children quickly heaped them into a glittering mound at the door.

"Come on," said Finn. "Now we're going to hide behind the costumes and wait for the cats."

They barely had time to hide before the door opened. Yowling hideously, the black cats streamed into the room. Then the door closed and locked.

"Let them come sniffing for us," Finn whispered. "Then when I give the signal, we'll tug these costumes down to the floor."

The frightful animals sniffed right and left. Their nasty claws clicked on the floor like teeth chattering on a frigid day.

"Now, Chloe!" shouted Finn.

The children yanked down the costumes and suddenly the glass sun on the boy's chest shot out rays of blazing light, reflecting the sparkle from the pile of jewels. Blinded, the cats ran for cover.

Listening at the door, the King of Night was impatient. Why weren't the children crying out in fear? He ordered the demons to open the door. They obeyed and he was instantly dazzled by the beams of the glass sun. Stumbling blindly into the sparkling mound, he sent gems and pearls flying every which way.

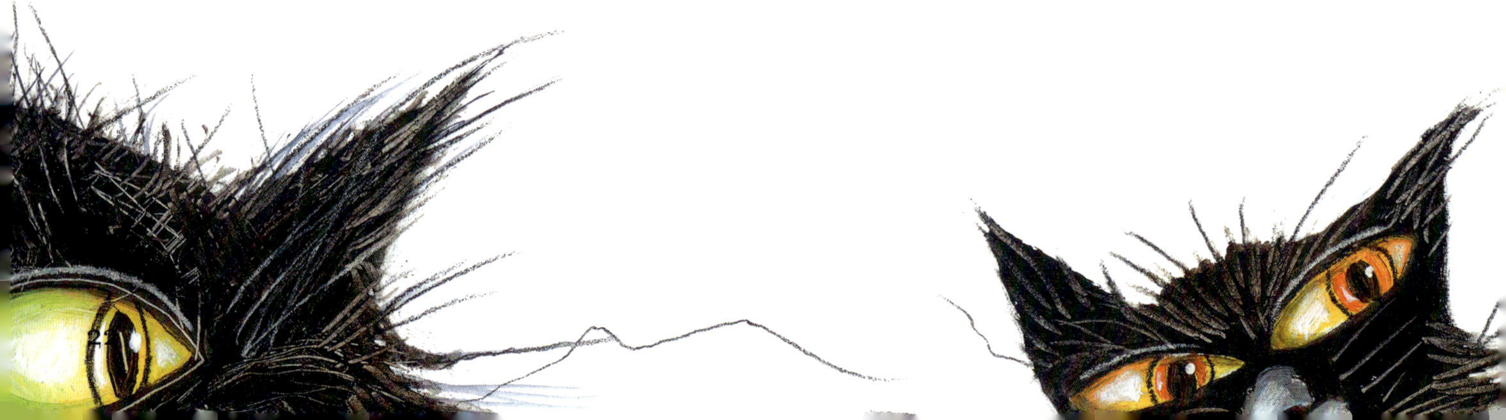

I feel a fit of anger escalating
A vein in my forehead is pulsating
I was very nice and sweet to you
And you chose to ignore the dark King of the Night!

I thought that in your head that's full of pride
would knock some sense, convince you to comply
One of my repulsive stinky demons
DO YOU KNOW WHO I AM?
THE DARK KING OF THE NIGHT!

I invited you to come over and meet me
But in my pretty house you have deceived me
You have chased away my fluffy kitties
HOW DARE YOU, DO THAT? To the dark King of the Night!

You've seen how nice and pleasant I can be
But now my angry side is the last you'll ever see!
Don't even begin to think of what awaits you
NO ONE CAN ESCAPE, FROM THE DARK KING OF THE NIGHT
NO ONE CAN ESCAPE
NO ONE CAN ESCAPE
NO ONE!

"Take these children to my float and tie them up good and tight!" the angry King roared.

Meanwhile, Henry and Emily, frantic with worry, had gone to find the Queen of Day. She was seated on a white throne atop her Carnival float, surrounded by her costumed army of animals and birds. There were eagles, sparrows, nightingales, seagulls, lions, bears, badgers, hares and many more.

Seeing the parents' desperate faces, the kindly old woman asked, "What's the matter?"

"The King of Night's demons have kidnapped our children, Finn and Chloe," gasped Henry.

"And we don't know where they've taken them," sobbed Emily.

"Don't worry," said the Queen of Day. "Trust me. We will find them."

Eagle, lion, hare and seagull soaring high,
I summon you to court
The dark King of the Night we have to capture,
His cruel evil plans at once we must cut short
I'm sending you to quickly look around,
And search in every corner of the town
You have to ask around a lot,
Sneak in every goblin shop
Careful that you don't get caught
And somewhere, somewhere,
Surely the children will be found!

I trust your sense of duty, you're always by my side
What would I do without you?
To whom confide?

Eagle, lion, hare and seagull soaring high,
Don't waste any time
We must find Finn and Chloe
Their sweet parents are worried sick so come on,
Bring them by my side
I know you can climb up any stair,
And find the King's secluded moldy lair
You have to ask around a lot,
And sneak in every goblin shop
Be careful that you don't get caught
And somewhere, somewhere,
Surely the children will be found!

The children had been carried off and tied to a column in the belly of the King of Night's float. But not without kicking and biting their captors along the way.

The float was immense, as big as an ocean liner and entirely black. Flames shot from various openings and black smoke billowed from a tall smokestack. Up top, costumed soldiers were milling around, some crawling, some dragging their tails, others flicking their tongues, and still others pretending to fly with the little wings stuck on their backs. Down below, watched by the anxious children, the demons were stoking a furnace with coal. The fire heated water in a boiler, the boiler made steam, and the steam powered the float through the streets.

The Queen sent the eagle, the seagull, the hare and the lion to scour the city. Questioning everyone they met, they finally found revelers who had seen the children slung over the demons' backs and learned where they had been taken.

Inside the float, the King of Night was planted in front of the children. His face was dark.

"Little girl," he said to Chloe, "I can see you are proud of your costume. Well, you won't be so proud after I cut it to shreds!"

He put out a hand to tear a magnificent cyclamen flower from her costume.

"That would be a pity," said Chloe. "If you looked closely at the flower, you would learn the secret of my costume. Because even without fancy fabrics, my mother knows what makes a cyclamen a cyclamen."

You can ask, if you want, you will never know
Mysteries, secret things
Like the ones that never have been told
All that glitters is not always made of gold
Only true love never can be bought and sold

Search one time, search again, search another time,
Look inside, look out there, you won't find it anywhere
'Cause you're looking in the places that it's not
Only true love puts the glitters in your heart

The King examined the flower more carefully.

"I don't see anything! Nothing but rags stitched with thread."

But he decided not to tear it off. Instead, he called for his tailors to see if they could discover the secret.

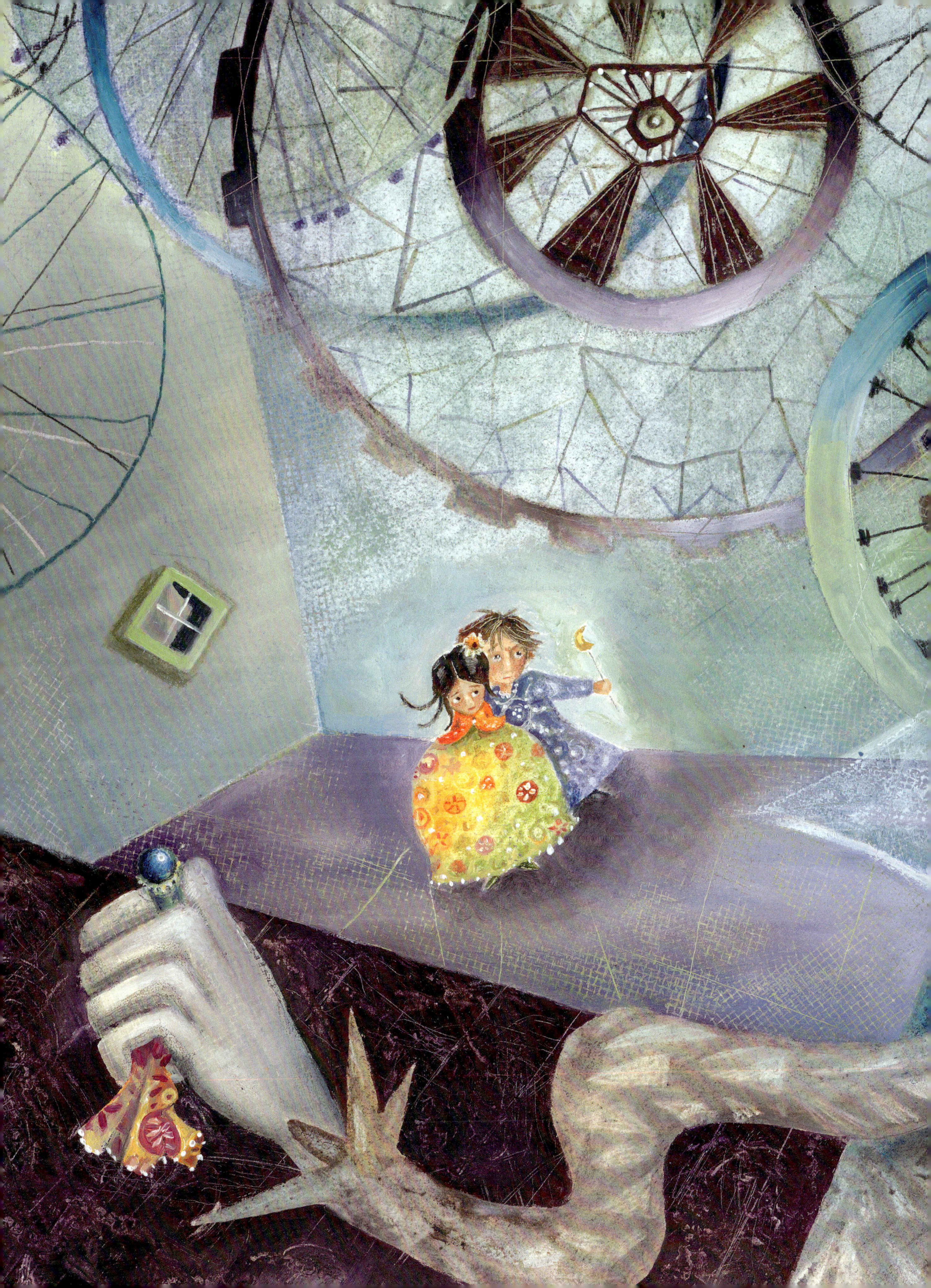

Turning to Finn, he said, "And you, my boy, you seem to be very proud of your costume. Let's see if you're still as proud after I pull the stars off, one by one.

The King of Night reached out to rip off a star.

"That would be a pity," said Finn. "If you looked closely at the star, you would learn the secret of my costume. Because even without precious stones, my mother knows what makes a star a star."

The King took a good look at the star. But he saw nothing, just bits of glass sewn on with thread. He decided not to pull it off, though. He would wait for his tailors to study it and discover the secret. In any event, it was time to punish the children.

"Blacken the boy with coal," he ordered the demons.

"And what if you dirty my costume?" said Finn. "If you blacken even one cotton cloud you will never learn the secret."

"Cut off the girl's braids," commanded the King of Night.

"And what if the scissors accidentally cut off a flower?" said Chloe. "If even one flower is lost you will never learn the secret."

"Enough nonsense! Take off their clothes and roll them in soot and cut off their hair," bellowed the furious King.

The demons untied the children. One carried over a bucket of soot and another a pair of scissors.

"Be brave, Chloe!" whispered Finn.

At that very moment, a battle erupted. The Army of Day stormed the King's float without warning, wrenching open the trap door and rushing inside.

Pandemonium

The dark float is overturning
Looks like a ship that's run ashore
Its oils have started burning
Steam and smoke rise in the air
It looks like all-out war
The eagle with his sharp beak attacks a wretched imp
And a scaly gremlin is moaning and has begun to limp
The donkey kicks a demon, look at that foolish wimp!
Roaring, the lion joins the fight, biting with force that goblin's hip

The battle is raging all around us
The King is screaming in distress
Clawing, and mauling, trampling, tearing
But who will escape
Who will escape
Who will escape from this big mess?
The Queen advances her armies
Imps are abandoning their King
He looks like he's exploding
He huffs and puffs and suffocates
What else could this day bring?
The demons are jumping wildly, they run away in fear
They're hiding in the chimney, here come the lion and the deer
In this total chaos the monkeys start to cheer
They're laughing at the goblins, the silly end of their career

The battle is raging all around us

When the battle ended, the defeated demons were herded into a corner with their clothes in tatters. Some of the animals seized the King of Night and led him to the Queen of Day. Others picked up the children and returned them to their parents, who hugged them and kissed them again and again.

Shame on you!
Our citizens are watching
Your dumb and empty noggin
I never would have thought that it could generate, such an evil plan
I'm crushing your ambition and ending your dark mission
Take these scrawny goblins…and vanish!
Go teach them to be useful, and not hurt anyone

My dearest Madame
Believe me, it's all a big mistake
My sweetest Madame
They only came over for some cake
My demons were baking (with their rosy cheeks)
The children just wanted to drop by and say hello to me

Lies lies lies

Shame on you!
Your soul is like a bog
Your breath stinks like a hog
Take him! I don't want to lay eyes on this blackened and shriveled rotten prune
When you do appear, everything you smear
Round up all your black cats… and flee!
Why don't you show them how to catch a rat from time to time?

My dearest Madame
Believe me, it's all a big mistake
My sweetest Madame
They only came over for some cake

The children decided (look at them sweeties!)
To visit and play all night, with my cute cats

Lies lies lies

Shame on you!

"Shame on you!" said the Queen of Day to the King of Night, who hung his head. "This time you've gone too far. What were you thinking, kidnapping these children? The Carnival needs you, but this year you are barred. Go! You're just too mean!"

Then, turning to Finn and Chloe, she said, "The parade is about to begin. Dance, have fun and don't be afraid of anything."

The fool of the Carnival we're chasing
He's the one we're chasing
He's the one we're chasing
He's the one we're chasing
Dance with us and hop onto our carrousel that's creaking

Anyone who thinks that we are joking
On our carrousel we won't be taking
Anyone who thinks that we are joking
On our carrousel we won't be taking

Let's go to the Carnival together
Let's all go together
Let's all go together
Let's all go together
Ride our fastest horse and get to town
We'll have fair weather

Anyone who does not like our teasing
In our lovely garden won't be staying
Anyone who does not like our teasing
In our lovely garden won't be staying

The parade of floats and costumes was truly extraordinary. And Henry, Emily and the children had fun dancing and singing happily for the rest of the day.

The Carnival was doubly unforgettable that year because, as they headed back to their village, when they were almost home, the whole family had to get out of the car and push it. For the engine had died halfway up the hill ... and no amount of coaxing could make it start again.

The Carnival of Marvels and Monsters

| 52:22 |

Overture*	1:27
On the way to the city**	1:09
Carnival*	2:29
The Queen of Day and the King of Night**	0:59
The Queen's lullaby*	2:16
Dressed as Sky and Earth**	0:54
The costumes*	2:46
Carnival commotion**	0:45
Polka*	1:05
Kidnapped!**	4:09
The black cats*	1:43
The King is angry**	0:39
What have we got here?*	2:11
Finn and Chloe imprisoned**	3:06
The costume room*	2:01
Finn courageous**	2:17
A fit of anger escalating*	1:46
The black float of terror **	1:04
Eagle lion hare*	2:07
The Queen takes action**	2:29
The secret*	2:05
Children defiant**	2:13
Pandemonium!*	2:55
Victory for the Queen**	0:22
Shame on you!*	3:38
The dark King chastised**	0:30
The Carnival fool*	2:13
The unforgettable feast**	0:48

* Giannis Georgantelis
** Mihalis Makropoulos

CD CREDITS

Orchestre symphonique pop de Montréal

VIOLINS
Nayiri Piloyan
Amélie Denoncourt
Caroline Beauchamp
Chon-Ho Lu
Darcie Hum
Joyce Blond
Judith Bichai
Marguerite Comley
Sonia Sara Théberge

VIOLAS
Sarah Ouellet
Lise Lambert
Hélène Blanchet

CELLOS
Olivier Caron
Karine Bouchard
Mallory Georges

BASSES
Martin Roy
Nicolas Belpaire

PIANO
Hélène Carrière

FLUTE
Michelle Moreau

CLARINET
Mélanie Paré

OBOE
Sean-Paul O'Brien

FRENCH HORNS
Tessa Hamilton
Michèle Rossong

TRUMPETS
Alexis Anderson
Nils Ek

TROMBONES
François Lefebvre
Alain Talbot

TUBA
Sabrina Boulanger

TIMPANI
Lanny Levine

PERCUSSION
Stéphane Savaria
Joann Blondin
Valérie Laville
Olivier Maranda

CONDUCTOR
Mark Dharmaratnam

FOUNDING PRESIDENT
Stéphane Savaria

Musicians – Athens

ACCORDION, PERCUSSION AND SYNTHESIZERS, GUITAR SOUNDS, SOUND EFFECTS
Giannis Georgantelis

GUITAR AND PERCUSSION
Makis Papagavriil

ELECTRIC BASS
Apostolos Kaltsas

The Sir Wilfrid Laurier School Board Choir

Jules Verne: Alejandro Gutierrez, Joy Chai • *Franklin Hill*: Alessia Rotiroti, Lily-Rose Tremblay • *Hillcrest*: Amisha Sebastiampillai, Anastasia Tsantes, Ayden Floyd, Dalia Linhares, Dimitri Pelekoudis, Georgia-Melina Theopoulos, Ileana Daduryan, Iliana Malamadakis, Juliana Scardera, Kyahna Beauchamp, Leah Andradi, Marianna Aravanis, Marianna Mecca, Matthew Chrzanowski, Maxwell Rager, Melina Simpson, Stavy Mathioudakis, Steliani Xydous, Syriana Gray, Yara Titrit Peddle-Omary • *Souvenir*: Demitra Demi Rokas, Zoe Ferri, Nancy Bilios • *JFK*: Maya Zahabi, Sandra Zahabi • *St-Vincent*: Maria Nicole Piperni, Michael Piperni • *McCaig*: Valentina Ryzewski Kleinubing, Rosalie Hedges • *Twin Oaks*: Caleb Johnston • *St. Paul*: Fiona Cutrona *Laval Junior*: Elena Despotopoulos • *Morin Heights*: Julia Vourantonis • *St. Jude*: Kaena Roy • *Crestview*: Kalliopi Mantzioros • *Lake of Two Mountains*: Maïa Marino • *OLP*: Sarah Rebecca Faria

Guest Schools

Socrate-Démosthène: Alexandra Karagioules, Aphrodite Georgaros, Cleo Mandros, Elena Kritikos, Eliana Meligrigoris, Emmanuela Kritikos, Katerina Stathopoulos, Lea Elenakis, Maria Ferlaino, Nicoletta Moschopoulos, Stavroula Vlaholias, Yorgo Girgi, Zoe Tourlas • *Chroma Musika Studio*: Christina Mihalakos, Despina Paschalidis, Gloria Wang, Han Hui

Cedarcrest Elementary School Choir

Principal: Civita Tudino

Adryanna-Victoria Usman, Amelia Pimentel, Amy Botsis, Arwyn Azcona, Ayo Hamilton Choy, Bianca Petrini, Destiny Spence,Emma Champod, Gabriel Piccirilli, Gabrielle Champod, Isabelle Trudeau, Janaya Mohan, Jeremy Riccardi, Julian Sarli, Karina Garcia Fasone, Laura Etrusco R. Moreira, Lilian Issa el Khoury, Madison Ghorayeb, Manny Becker, Maria Isabella Fercher, Maria Stefanakis, Matea Pimentel, Oceana Lola Sierra Torres, Oliver Johnstone, Oliver Mackenzie Gee, Ophelia Barile, Panagiota Michalarias, Roxanne Anderson, Sara Riccardi, Stephanie Mourelatos, Theodora Vlachos, Tyniah Alexander, Vanessa Cucci, Vasiliki, Simeonidis

Edinburgh Elementary School Choir

Principal: Mauro Zampini

Alessia Rivera, Annabelle Demaine, Augusten Walz, Ava Salkovitz, Caitlin Matheson Lunt, Cecilia Samayoa, Christina Vietri, Ella Siné Wilson, Emilie Love, Emrik Blondin, Isabella Zagari, Justin Rodger, Kaitlyn Friedman, Madeleine Edwards-Martinez, Malina Hakien, Maya Di Fazio, Mhairi Scanlon, Mia Srna Pasagic, Miia D'Addio, Naseelah Nebebe, Nola Bédard, Nora Allan, Olive Violini-Heisler, Phoenix Blondin, Sigrid A.Scott Rodriguez, Solana Ramos, Taryn Cleghorn, Tori Mannix, Zara Currie

Gardenview Elementary School Choir

Principal: Demetra Droutsas, Vice Principals: Gaetano Sifoni and Eugenia Carystios

Adam Arui, Akshay Kakkar, Alessia Marquez Borelli, Alexa Hamou, Alexandra Athanasopoulos, Alexandra Turk, Alexia Fagnani, Alexia Matassa, Anabelle Daoud, Andrianna Kolovos, Angeliki Kabiotis, Annabelle Aizanman, Anthony Tarasco, Aristea Karras, Brooklynne Anderson, Cleo Kountourakis, Daniel Benarroch, Emma Silveira, Gabriella Mura, Giada Stabile, Giovanna Karam, Huda Runjeet, Isabella Kouchakdjian, Isabella Vergara-Pardo, Jade Prowse, Juliana Vitoroullis, Katherine Del Torto, Kayla Ferguson, Leila Minh Tran, Liviana Lopez, Luciana Vargas, Maya Benarroch, Melina Avdeliodis, Melissa Nguyen, Mila Coirazza, Natasha Langevin-Bouthillier, Noa Zeitoune, Olivia Jay, Olivia McFarlane, Olivier Chiotis, Rebecca Elkoubi, Sabrina Botelho, Sara Bianchini, Sara Corsi, Serena Zaccagnini, Sienna Elias, Sienna Lopez, Sofia Mezzacappa, Sofia Stamatiou, Stefanie Arvanitis, Sydney Kaufman, Velessa Kagan, Victoria Kouchakdjian, Yael Rosenzweig

Honoré Mercier Elementary School Choir

Principal: Sonia Marotta, Vice Principal: Christina Voggas

Alexa Calabrese, Angelina Cucuzzella, Clara Di Marco, Emily Wong, Eva Rosa Nardi, Isabella D'Anello, Kaylynn Langlois, Keira Vijh, Liana Spiratos, Michael Tilli, Nina Seminara, Sara Murgante, Simona Gioffre, Simona Schiro

Pierre de Coubertin Elementary School Choir

Principal: Ida Pisano

Adriana Di Lalla, Alexia Tutino, Alyssia Bédard, Angelina D'Amico, Antonia Angelina Lisella, Camelia Fata Allegrezza, Camilla Fata Allegrezza, Carmela Falduto, Dante Manco, Elisa Montoro, Emma Rinaldi, Eva Colabelli, Eva Manocchio, Eva Mazzilli, Felicia Morrone, Gabriella Varricchio, Gia Iannotti, Gianna Vigna, Giulia Maietta, Hailey P. Medeiros, Hailey Tutino, Julia Pomponi, Kayla Insogna, Layla Vu, Lea Ly, Lia Mazzilli, Lily Rose Conciatori, Lorenzo Martiniello, Mikela Pagano, Nathanyl Monachino, Olivia Catenaccio, Sabrina Ben, Sara Colabelli, Sean Repapis, Shivaa Tuknat Gandhi, Siena Palmieri, Sienna Malky, Vanessa Victoria Lisella

Roslyn Elementary School Choir

Principal: Joanna Genovezos, Vice Principal: Danica J. Lewington

Alessia Di Gennaro, Bahar A.R., Beatrice Reynolds, Brooke Looper, Camila Mejia Place, Charlotte MacKinnon, Chloe Giambagno, Daphne Loane-Billings, Denver Ly, Dylan Miao, Emerson Gilbert Jacquart, Emma Blundell, Eve Bercuvitz, Florence Bettez, Halia Souweine, Hazel Lenz, Isabel Davies, Kesenya Kennedy, Kiara Davidson, Leen Nazer, Lorena Mandri Lugo, Lubna Alzahrani, Meftaha Slaoui, Mélanie Béïque, Menna Hussein, Mia Feng, Mikaila Maria Tilden, Mila Khozieva, Millie Dudley, Natalia Mandri Lugo, Nicholas Maniatis, Noa Ellbogen-Deschamps, Océane Tilden, Olivia Carmosino, Rafla Bencheik, Rhianna Islam, Rose Landis, Sabrina Tilden, Sally Kim, Savanna Fredovitch Filippone, Selena Ramsey, Sienna Therrien Sternfeld, Simona Makkerh, Sophia Mahar, Stephanie Paz, Tala Nieto-Castro, Vasili Polymenakos, Victoria Arcaro, Victoria Duroseau, Yara Alzahrani, Yeseul Kang

Royal Vale Elementary School Choir

Principal: Nathalie Lacroix-Maillette, Vice Principal: Saverio Servello

Alyssa Perez, Anais Poppe, Caroline Mandoiu-Puscasu, Charlotte Gyetvay-Cruz, Christian Lobaugh, Daniel Joven-Alberto, Devina Niyogi, Eden Osbourne, Eliane Levary Goldstein, Elora Finegan, Emilie Wan, Emma McCarthy, Eva Rotili, Eva Thouret, Hannah Flacks, Joanne Collamat, Jonathan Abraham Tordjman, Jonathan Goldstein, Jude George, Kathie Wei, Kenya Cartier-Bruckert, Kristen Noble, Kylee Frankel, Lauren Shanahan, London Parise, Mackenzie Caron, Maggie Wan, Malaika O'Connor-Aversa, Mary Sy, Mia De Paola, Mia Korngold, Momo Kamiki, Nikolai Konieczny, Olivia Hilal-Gervais, Olivia Ortaaslan, Olivia Park, Pearl Acheng, Raphaele Simsovic, Riley Croll, Sarah Zelman, Shimon Kamiki, Sophie Eiser, Sophie Small, Sorayah Barhone, Spencer Garzon, Sterling McGregor, Talia Leblanc, Waka Hashimoto, Zoë Di Francesco, Zuleica Seoeun Cheon

St. Monica Elementary School Choir

Principal: Silvana Crigna

Aiden Han, Aminah Dahman, Anaya Hinkson, Aria Solimene, Armin Moradi, Brianna-Kassandra Liz-Perez, Cicek Arslan, Daniela Güemez Beauregard, Ebony Colley-Sinare, Eleanore Drvar, Emma Paynter-Khitab, Jaeyoon Chung, John Byun, Katherine Kim, Mia Zuniga, Mikayla Cartier, Nolan Semienchuk, Oscar Cornish, Pilar Bacelar Munoz Monteiro Dos Santos, Roxanne Ross, Shanaya Milind Marathe, Skye-Raphael Ali, Stéphanie Jouliette, Houalla Otero

Willingdon Elementary School Choir

Principal: Carmen Nicolas, Vice Principal: Steve Spetsieris

Aliyah Healey-Mungo, Atom Chauvin, Charlie Rae Rittenhouse, Chiara Granata, Corinne Taylor, Dalia Chioda, Daphnée Bélanger, Emma Cavanagh-Themelis, Emma Chioda, Emma Etezadi-Barron, Emma Ni, Fabio Ninzatti, Hae in On, Jasmine Peters, Justin Melville, Kaya Cowper, Liliana Grey, Lily Covington, Lily-Anne Darbyson, Madison McGravie, Maximillian Curiel-Ploumis, Melissah Cain, Meredith Headon, Nola Caslini, Rose MacRae, Seren Brady, Simone Peters, Sophie McCalla, Sydney Ross

Choir Soloists (reference voices)

Nicholas Maniatis, Amy Botsis, Oliver Mackenzie Gee, Fiona Cutrona, Alessia Rotiroti, Gloria Wang, Han Hui, Joy Chai, Alexandra Athanasopoulos

Soloists "Pandemonium" and "Costume Room"

Amy Botsis, Oliver Mackenzie Gee, Fiona Cutrona, Christina Mihalakos, Alessia Rotiroti, Gloria Wang, Han Hui, Joy Chai, Eliana Meligrigoris, Anabelle Daoud, Alexandra Turk, Alexandra Athanasopoulos, Fabio Ninzatti, Ioustini Motzenigos, Despina Paschalidis, Kalliopi Mantzioros and the 5th and 6th grade choristers of Roslyn Elementary School

Cast

NARRATOR: Susan Bain
QUEEN OF DAY: Maria Diamantis
KING OF NIGHT: Dimitris Ilias
CHLOE: Alexandra Karagioules
FINN: David Flexer
GOBLIN VOICES: Matea Pimentel

Production

COMPOSITION, ORCHESTRATION AND SCORES
Giannis Georgantelis
ORIGINAL LYRICS
Giannis Georgantelis
MUSIC PRODUCTION
Chroma Musika
EDUCATIONAL PROGRAMS
Panarmonia Atelier Musical
ARTISTIC AND MUSICAL DIRECTION
Maria Diamantis and Dimitris Ilias
STORY TRANSLATION AND ADAPTATION
Marcia Couëlle
SONG TRANSLATION AND ADAPTATION
Dimitris Ilias and Maria Diamantis
CHOIRMASTERS
Dimitris Ilias and Maria Diamantis (Edinburgh, Willingdon, Gardenview, Cedarcrest, Pierre de Coubertin, Honoré Mercier, Roslyn, Royal Vale and Sir Wilfrid Laurier School Board)
Christine Liautaud (St. Monica)
RECORDING AND MIX, ORCHESTRA AND CHOIR
Mark Corwin, PhD
RECORDING, NARRATOR
Dimitris Ilias, Chroma Musika
RECORDING, SOLOISTS
Dimitris Ilias, Chroma Musika
MIXING
Studio Praxis
MASTERING
Productions AEM (Montreal)
STUDIOS
Oscar Peterson Concert Hall (Montreal)
Chroma Musika (Montreal)
Productions AEM (Montreal)
VOLUNTEERS AND SUPERVISOR COORDINATOR
Lysanne Abelardo
FUNDRAISING COORDINATOR
Jaimie Auger
PRODUCTION DOCUMENTARY
Lysanne Abelardo

Chroma Musika and Panarmonia Atelier Musical wish to thank the following sponsors, partners and individuals for their immense support.

Partners

The English Montreal School Board
The Sir Wilfrid Laurier School Board
The Hellenic Community of Greater Montreal

Sponsors and Supporters

Platinum Circle - Friends of the Carnival

Hon. Marwah Rizqy (MNA for Saint-Laurent)

Gold Circle - Friends of Chloe

Hon. Jennifer Maccarone (MNA for Westmount-Saint-Louis)
Hon. Kathleen Weil (MNA for Notre-Dame-de-Grâce)
Mrs. Mary Deros (City Councilor for Park Extension)
Bijouterie Santorini - Razmick Nazarian and Stacey Eftaxias
Bouquet St. Laurent - Joseph Botelho
Club d'enfants jeu t'aime - Dora Stea and Marco Coirazza

Silver Circle - Friends of Finn

Hon. Filomena Rotiroti (MNA for Jeanne-Mance-Viger)
FL Fuller Landau SENCRL/LLP
Hon. Francine Charbonneau (MNA for Mille-Îles)
Guy Ouellette (MNA for Chomedey)
Manu Kakkar, BSc. (Hons), MTax, TEP, CPA, CA, President, Manu Kakkar CPA Inc.
Vicky Georgiadou, Certified Real Estate Broker, QSC, and Nancy Zentefis, Real Estate Broker
Despina Ioanidis, official photographer

Special thanks to:

All our amazing parent volunteers!
Senator Leo Housakos, the Hon. Jennifer Maccarone, the Hon. Guy Ouellette (MNA for Chomedey), Nicholas Pagonis (President Hellenic Community of Greater Montreal), Angela Mancini (President EMSB), Paolo Galati (Chairperson SWLSB), Vicky Kaliotzakis (Vice-Chairperson SWLSB), Guy Gagnon (Commissioner SWLSB), Ann Marie Matheson (DG EMSB), Chris Adamopoulos (DG École Socrates-Démosthène), Frédéric Greschner (ADG SWLSB), Pelagia Nickoletopoulos (Regional Director EMSB), Evelyne Alfonsi (Regional Director EMSB), Geoffrey Hipps (DPS SWLSB), Michael Quinn (ADPS SWLSB), Lysanne Abelardo, Jaimie Auger, Christine Long (CTV News), Robert Ostiguy and Andrea Howick (Global TV), Michael Tellides (CFMB 1280 AM), George Guzmas (Newsfirst), Zuleika Seoeun Cheon, parents of Caleb Johnston, the Tabag-Collmart Family, Peter Auger and Susan Auger, Le Ste Rose - Dimitri Aravanis, Piano Vertu - Maxime Séguin, Radu Covaciu, Stephan Globensky, Maria Lazaris, Louise Robineau, and all the families of our young songbirds for their dedication.

Planète rebelle
P.O. Box 55049 Fairmount
Montreal, Quebec H2T 3E2 CANADA
514 278 7375
www.planeterebelle.qc.ca

Éditions Planète rebelle gratefully acknowledges support for its publishing program from the Canada Council for the Arts, Société de développement des entreprises culturelles du Québec (SODEC) and the Government of Québec – Tax credit for book publishing – Administered by SODEC.

We also acknowledge the financial support of the Government of Canada through the Canada Book Fund for our publishing activities.

Publisher: Marie Fleurette Beaudoin
Translator, story: Marcia Couëlle
Translators, songs: Dimitris Ilias and Maria Diamantis
Graphic design: Marie-Eve Nadeau
Distribution: Diffusion Dimedia www.dimedia.com

Original Greek title: Το Καρναβάλι των Θαυμάτων και των Τεράτων
Published in French as Le Carnaval des merveilles et des monstres
Authorized by: Chroma Musika

Legal deposit: 4th quarter 2019
Bibliothèque et Archives nationales du Québec
Library and Archives Canada

Cataloguing in Publication Data
Bibliothèque et Archives nationales du Québec
Library and Archives Canada

Title: The Carnival of Marvels and Monsters / Mihalis Makropoulos
Names: Makropoulos, Mihalis, 1965- author. | Georgantelis, Giannis, 1963- composer. | Veroutsou, Katerina, 1957- illustrator. | Couëlle, Marcia, 1943-, Diamantis, Maria, 1965-, Ilias, Dimitris, 1969- translators.
Series: Des mots plein la bouche | Translated from French. | Accompanied by a compact disc.
Target audience: Children age 5 and up
Identifiers: Canadiana (print) 20190019344 | Canadiana (ebook) 20190019352 |
ISBN 9782924797457 (hardcover) | ISBN 9782924797488 (PDF)
Subjects: LCSH: Operas—Juvenile—Librettos.
Classification: LCC ML50.G46 C3713 2019 | DDC j782.1026/8— dc23

Printed by Transcontinental Printing
in September 2019

Imprimé au Canada • Printed in Canada